Human

Breaking, Healing and Flourishing

Jayden O'Hara

Tellwell Talent
www.tellwell.ca

ISBN
978-0-2288-4291-0 (Paperback)
978-0-2288-4292-7 (eBook)

Dedicated to all of life's experiences, to the ones who come and go, to the ones still learning to love themselves. to the ones in love, to the ones falling apart.

This one's for you.

To the one's searching for something
beautiful in this world,
Look within,
It was you all along.

My first love was poetry,
Years later,
Every time the pen touched the paper,
Grazing my lover's skin,
I'm still speechless…

    –   Writer's block

Poetry is only spoken when raw feeling drips from your lips,

Otherwise you're speaking colourful sentences.

–   The truth

Poetry

Definition: A messy letter compiled of raw words torn from
the heart,
A bloody string of words,
Like tearing a seam from denim,
It's left a little frayed.

A Poet

Definition: A human being with a soul brave enough to
display his or her frayed heart in a glass case, demonstrating
the feelings of love, heartache, fear and joy.

A messy letter + a messy person
=
A beautiful piece of art depicting every ounce of love,
heartache, fear and joy felt.

Always appreciate a soft woman,
For her heart is filled with all of the riches you could wish for.

Her softness caught your eye early on.
Her kind heart, gentle eyes and most of all, her burning desire
to fill her soul passionately with elegance and femininity.

Softness should be welcomed,
As it allows beauty, elegance and kindness to flow throughout
the earth.

Summer nights when the stars come out.
When the clouds clear away, and the colourful lights dance
about the night.

Eloquent colours from green to pink,
Reflect over the water.

As the night lingers, it will all disappear in a blink.
As the entire sky illuminates in brilliant colours,
The constellations join in the nightly dance,
As if the sky is painted with water colours.

The sun begins to rise,
And an unseasoned day is born.
Now the night falls asleep,
Until the dancing sky returns,
The earth awakens once more

The end was only the beginning,
Where she turned her darkest past,
Into the brightest future
Sadness became joy,
Silence became laughter.

Her new chapter began,
Wild as the blossoming flowers.
She lived with elegance,
Wandered with imagination
And loved with all her heart.

The love she showed herself,
Overflowed to those around her.
She grew stronger and more capable,
Emerging above the fire that surrounded her
She has risen.

Your eyes remind me of an adventure that I have yet to begin.
With the hopes of not having an end.

The aroma of roasting coffee beans,
The quietest of fragrances.

The sounds of traffic swiftly passing,
blended with Lana Del Rey's Art Deco,
Is what I meditate to.

Paint splatters, Coffee stains and ink on paper have crafted
my beliefs as a creator and began the messy, chaotic process
of discovering one's self.

The simplest things in life are filled with the most joy and
reflect the most beauty.

The moment slumber creeps in,
Her mind drifts to the stars,
An infinite blaze,
And flowers waltzing in the wind.

Her most treasured place,
A place where she settles in
With a blanket, a hot cup of tea
And an empty canvas to paint the sunset.

But this indulgence will soon fade,
Until the haze of her sweet slumber
Is lifted and her deranged world
Comes back to life and she will long for that slumber.

You're like the ocean
Always sparkling,
Making me smile
When you touch my skin.

You're an adventure
I never want it to end.

Like a book I never want to finish,
That I could read over and over.

You're that rainy day,
That makes me want to curl up on the couch
And dance in the rain.
You are the love
I never want to leave.

He's learned pain,
But only knows love.
He's everything.
My love.

These scars show that I have lived,
I've cried myself to sleep at night,
I've worried about the things that don't matter.
I have loved

And been broken.

So why would I ever want to cover them up?

They're my war paint.

                    I'm ready.

I'm crazy about you
And somehow it makes me crazy enough to give everything
to you,
Even the power to break me

    It's all there.

Yet all you want to do is see me, hold me,

   Make me the happiest girl in the world.

And I love it.

Waking up early,
Messy bun, drinking tea,
Eating good food,
Not a drop of makeup.

I feel this buzz, this warmth,
I feel comfortable with myself,
I'm happy.

I show up for myself,
Kind, gentle, and taking my time.
And I'm finally where I want to be

She longed for the rain,
To sit in a car,
At a red light,
While moonlight spilled down the windows.

The traffic lights slowed the night
And painted a smile on your face.
When you looked at me,
I wanted to stay there forever.

The climax of the night,
Carried soft air,
And warm smiles,
All I needed was a kiss in the rain.

He kissed me,
And his hands,
Explored no further,
Then gently caressing my face.

To have your love surround me,

Even as I'm still fixing myself…

One by one I pick up the pieces,
The pieces he tore out of me
With every touch
And I never felt a thing,
Until he didn't want me,
He tore out the one seam
Which held every part of me together.

With each frayed edge and slanting curve,
You help me put the pieces back,
But not all of it fits,
I have grown stronger
And you still love every frayed edge
And missing piece.

Every one of us has a flaw,
Several flaws.
As if they're different markings.
Rather than comparing the markings,
We could bring them together,
To solve the puzzle.
Placing each piece where its meant to be

- We could change the world.

She's the kind of creative, up late burning the midnight oil, on her 4th cup of coffee, scribbling out poetry as it's flowing through her fingertips.

Her eyes are heavy, but her mind flourishes with thoughts. Her writing keeps her soul burning throughout the night, spilling over onto the pages around her.

Rain falls down the window, the droplets outlining the papers scattered all around her floor.
Steam rises from the coffee, as the air cools.

She smiles to herself, watching the sunrise.

A beautiful mess,
Like that heart-warming poem covered in coffee stains.

Like those faded overalls,
Frayed at the edges.

Like that heart
So frail,
So beautiful,
So messy.

You showed me what I didn't deserve, that I deserved more, you are the reason that I love myself more than I ever have.

Your leaving only brought joy and healing.

I used to search for you in others, now you're the last thing I want to find.

So, I just want to thank you for tossing me to the side, for making me feel like nothing,

Because I know I am a queen, who, all this time, already had a crown; my courage, I never needed you to give me that.

Sincerely, what was once yours,

  - The happiest girl in the world.

Some days we dream about our future,
Conspiring our life together,
Our apartment, our dog.

We talk about our kids,
How many,
And how we would raise them,
Giving them a childhood, they won't need to escape.

You look at me…
And I see it,
Just beneath the softness of your heart,

I wouldn't want that with anyone else.

<u>Blue</u>

A colour often foreshadowing sadness,
It may conflict with love.
Leaving a single teardrop,
Or heavy rainfall.

But that heavy downpour,
Brings young lovers to dance in the streets.
Drenched in fidelity,
Saturated in ecstasy.

A colour that may symbolize new life.
It could be the colour that shines when you gaze into her eyes
It's a display of joy in the sky on a sunny day.
It's relaxation as the waves tumble onto the shore.

Imagine a beautiful, blazing sunset,
Scattering pinks, purples and deep oranges among the
darkened clouds.

The summer heat hangs in the air,
The kind that leaves you wandering down to the beach,
Sipping on your favourite tea.
You admire how the sun slowly reaches to kiss the water
before fading into a vivid pastel aurora.

You're filled with a familiar feeling of euphoria, a childlike
wonder, forgetting to breathe for a moment,
Soaking up the stillness of the world.

You tiptoe down the rocky shore, dipping your toes in the
water.
The feeling sends a chill up your spine, surprising you with
a smile.

You close your eyes to listen to the water shuffle back and
forth from the pebbled shore.
A distant hum rises from a boat
making its final round, as if a
lullaby sends the beach back
to sleep.

You could have sworn,
The way she moved,
Brought the sun to its knees.

She was elegant, driven and burning with desire,
Suddenly her soul was on fire.

      – Self-acceptance

True happiness is when you allow yourself to learn every inch of your body and see its worth.
It's when you stop wanting to change and start wanting to live.

True happiness is when you embrace being soft and begin to connect to the world around you through your mind, body and soul.
It's when you learn to trust your own beautiful intuition.

I'm crazy about you
And somehow it makes me crazy enough to give everything
to you,
Even the power to break me

        It's all there.

Yet all you want to do is see me, hold me,

        Make me the happiest girl in the world.

And I love it.

You mean everything to me,

And there is nothing that could change that.

I love you.

Her elegance wasn't all glamour and rose-coloured glasses,

She lived in harmony with her body,
Delicately with her mind,
And fiercely with her soul.

As we drove down that backroad,
The sun shining, music blaring,
I couldn't keep myself from glancing at that smile.
And you singing along in a goofy voice,
Making me laugh.

We danced around in that golden field,
Your hands around my waist,
Looking into my eyes.

All I could think about was I wanted to tell you,
How far I've fallen,
For that smile, that laugh, the kindness in your eyes.

That's what I love,

You.

Life draws distance between the things you love.
Pick up that pen and write,
Just write.

   - A prescription for your soul

I spend my days building walls
Just to keep us safe.

I'll swallow the tears
And hold back the pain inside.

When my walls crack,
You may hear a cry for help,

Ignore it.

Don't trace it back to the wound
Because my walls will come crashing down,

And you'll leave because its messy,

And I'll be left to piece it back together,
Even higher than before.

Baggy sweaters,
Messy hair,
And the dark circles beneath her empty eyes.
She lost herself and can't seem to find her way back
But she's trying, with everything she has,
not to fall apart.
Fearing that she may never fit the pieces back together

She threw her head back laughing,
Taken in by a warm embrace,
Smiling...
By day.

She struggled, falling back to her invisible self,
Feeling lost,
With an empty gaze...
By night.

Little smiles fluttered through the hallways,
But they were blind,
She didn't matter,
She just wanted to feel okay again.

Even her happy, drunken self grew desperate
For anything...

Just one smile.

How did we get here?

One minute we're laughing, kissing, holding hands

And the next moment we haven't spoken in weeks

I loved you…

    Now I've lost you

I miss you.

The last of the bitter-sweet wine trickled off her lip,
As a tear rolled down her cheek.
She would soon rise to her low,
As dawn crept in the clock.

She'd play pretend,
A ragdoll,
Sew that fake smile back on,
Needle in hand,
Piercing her flesh.

That smile said everything
She didn't feel,
That everything was okay,
That everything was absolutely perfect.

My eyes are heavy,
But my mind is filled with too much chaos.

Isn't it the greatest feeling to be above everyone, outstretched,
on top of the world?
Just to abuse people with praise,
Only to mask who you really are.

The way you twist our minds, make us feel small, powerless
and selfish.

Afterall, I had you on a pedestal,
Was that me? How could I do such a wicked thing?
Exist as a young, naive girl who trusted you?
An absolute sinner, that is outrageous!

I can assure you that I have noted that,
An unfortunate mistake like that will never happen again,
I can promise you that.

Sound familiar?

Accusing me of being selfish, ungrateful and disloyal,
Because I'm afraid to trust you?
Afraid of the routine criticism because my life isn't suitable
to match your requirements.
And why does it matter to you?
I ask myself that everyday and I've drawn the conclusion that
there is no existing realistic answer to that question.

Only, the worst of it,
I'm left to grieve the loss of a person that never existed.

The night before we began,
You had pills in your mouth…
You were ready to let it all go.

After sitting in your room for days,
Muscles aching,

Your heart, aching…

But you never let go,
You were strong,
You stayed to fight another day
Something told you to spit them out.

Nearly a year later,
You're still here with me,
Still fighting
                              Everyday.

I couldn't be happier that you stayed for me.

You're so far away, calling to me,

But when I reach out, you disappear…

As if I'm nothing.

You've left me behind, tossed to the side
I'm lost.

With only the burden of myself, weighing me down.

I walk holding my head high and my cheek turned, but inside,

I can't hide it.

I've moved on but my heart still aches.

You know how to make me laugh, even if we're a million miles away from each other.

But you don't realize how much I cry because of you.

You're that one thing I want more than anything but I can't have because you bring more tears than laughter

and I hate that.

A sliver of moonlight slipped in through the window
Tracing out her silhouette.
Silence filled a room,
Where laughter was once heard.

The rain slowly creeps in
Through her eyes, where a sparkle remains so dim
Her heart mangled like the wallpaper tearing off the wall.

A cold coffee next to torn up roses is all that he left,
After he left…
Her broken.

Laying there, cold,
In a dim room, where bittersweet nostalgia lingered
She couldn't move, she couldn't breathe.
As if her insides were hollowed out.
The words spoken, scorched her bones cold,
The flame charred her insides.
She was empty.

But her heartbeat remained,
A tear down her cheek, the first sign of life.
Her breath cut through the blaring silence.
A halo of light flooded the room,
Silently, she smiled
She had a beautiful Smile.

Laying there, cold,
In a dim room, where bittersweet nostalgia lingered
She couldn't move, she couldn't breathe,
As if her insides were hollowed out.
The words spoken scorched her bones cold,
The flame charred her insides.
She was going to be okay.

You haunt me every night.
The thought of you,
Followed by my own demons.

But I've been strong this long,
I will keep going,
Until the very thought of you
Is erased.

Until I remember to forget you;

Your touch, your smell, your smile

All of you

Every memory of us laughing, fighting,
Just everything.

I hate that I loved you,
You live in every dream.

Drunk you said I was too fucking emotional

Drunk you said that you didn't know how to fucking deal
with me.

I laid my head back in my chair,

And watched the stars,

While tears rolled down my cheeks.

So that you wouldn't see.

There is newly created online community called
selfcare and coffee.

Visit this page on Instagram and click the blink in my bio
to join a growing community of poets, writers, readers and
everything else beautiful.
It is a discussion forum to bounce ideas off of each other, talk
about everything we love.
To put it simply, it is a community of positive vibes, organized
by myself.

Ps,

A friendly reminder to show up for yourself every day,
Whether that's sweatpants and coffee or dressing up and going out.
Drag yourself out of bed and drink a glass of water.
Start your day off with some yoga or stretching because your beautiful
body deserves to move, and your incredible mind deserves to release.

I Love You.

www.ingramcontent.com/pod-product-compliance
Lightning Source LLC
Chambersburg PA
CBHW051010050726
47592CB00007B/2788